DRAWING IS EASY!

I0902080

DRAWING ANIMALS

Written by Elizabeth Golding
Illustrated by Hui Yuan Chang
Designed by Anton Poitier

Published in 2022 by Windmill Books,
an Imprint of Rosen Publishing
29 East 21st Street, New York, NY 10010

Illustrated by: Hui Yuan Chang

Cataloging-in-Publication Data

Names: Golding, Elizabeth, author. | Chang, Hui Yuan, illustrator.
Title: Drawing animals / written by Elizabeth Golding, illustrated by Hui Yuan Chang.
Description: New York : Windmill Books, 2022. | Series: Drawing is easy!
Identifiers: ISBN 9781499487220 (pbk.) | ISBN 9781499487244 (library bound) | ISBN 9781499487237 (6 pack) | ISBN 9781499487251 (ebook)
Subjects: LCSH: Animals in art--Juvenile literature. | Drawing--Technique--Juvenile literature.
Classification: LCC NC780.G66 2022 | DDC 743.6--dc23

Printed in the United States of America

CPSIA Compliance Information: Batch BSWM22: For Further Information contact Rosen Publishing, New York, New York at 1-800-237-9932

WINDMILL BOOKS

Let's get started!

This book shows you how to draw animals by drawing shapes. There are steps to draw every animal. There are also lots of hints and tips for making your drawings different!

Get drawing!

1 Begin by drawing the first shape in the center of a piece of paper.

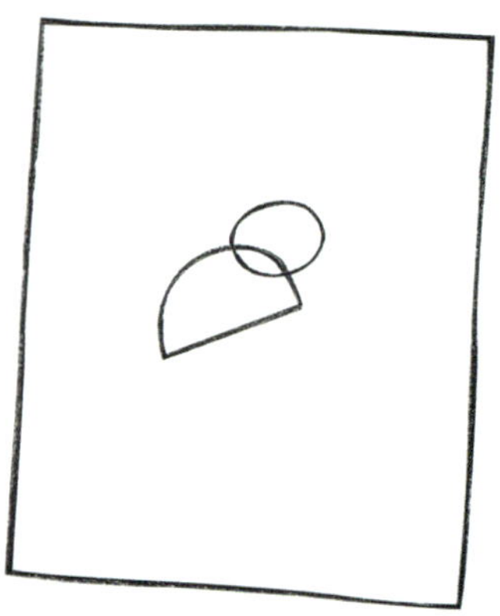

2 Next, draw the second shape where shown.

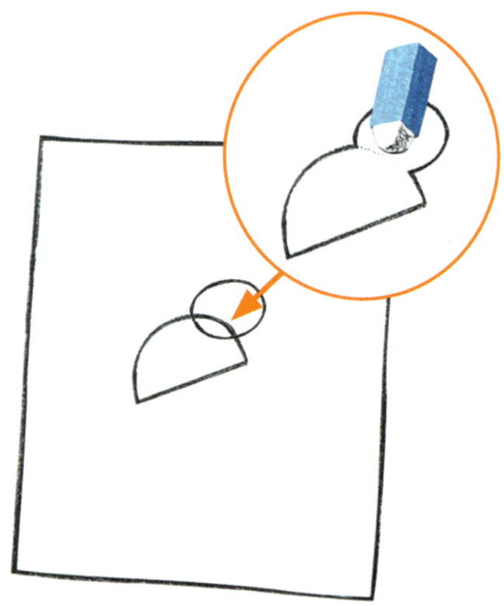

3 Use an eraser to erase the pencil marks where the shapes overlap.

Coloring tips to make your animal special

Coloring your pictures

Here are some handy tips. You can use colored pencils, felt-tip pens, crayons, or watercolor paints to complete your drawing. Water-soluble colored pencils work very well. The pictures in this book are colored in this way.

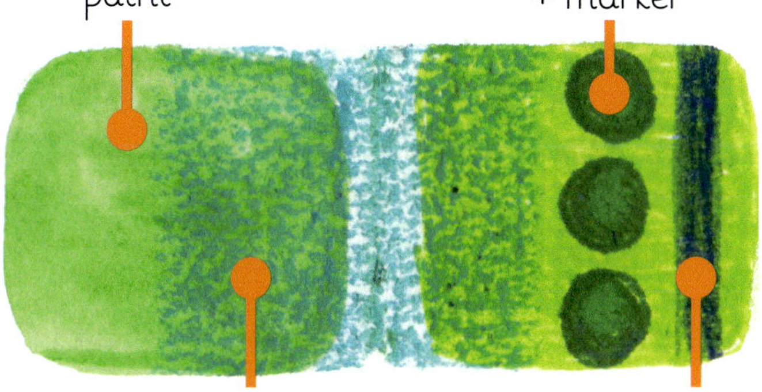

Draw a happy dog

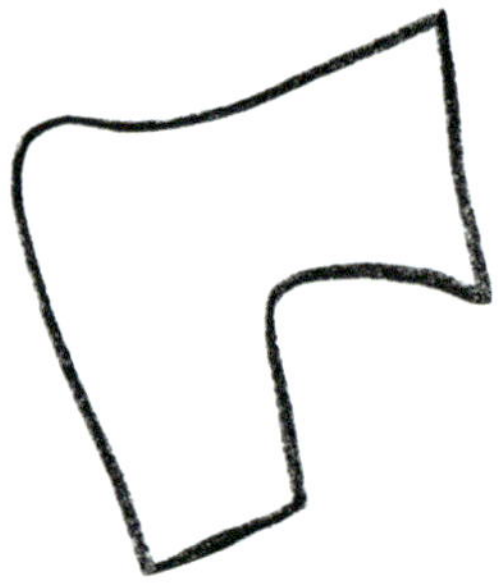

His head is facing backward.

1 Draw the dog's head.

2 Now draw the ears.

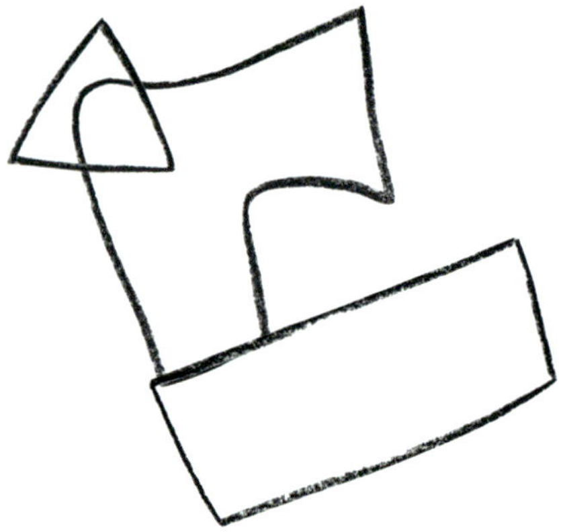

3 Add the body.

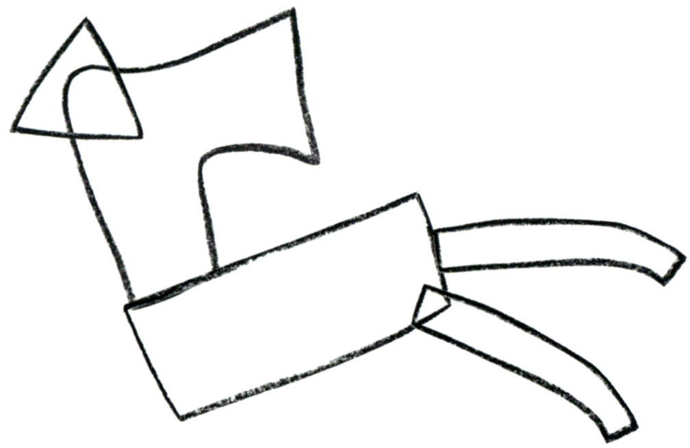

4 Draw the back legs.

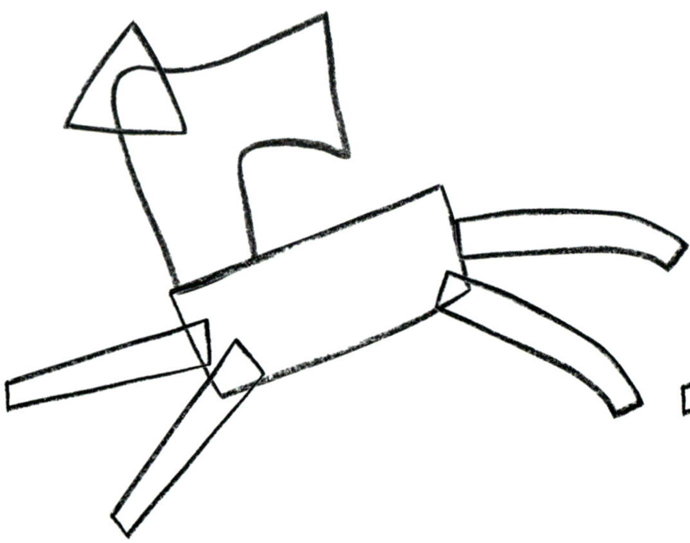

5 Add the front legs.

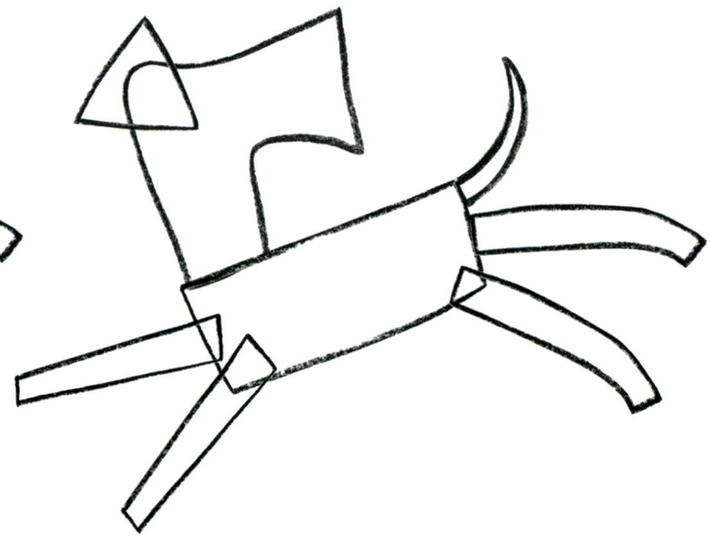

6 Add a curved tail.

Add a collar and ball too!

Make his tail wag!

Color your dog with paints or colored pencils.

Make your dog look different!

Draw a bone.

Head at an angle

Sitting up

Leaning forward to chase a ball

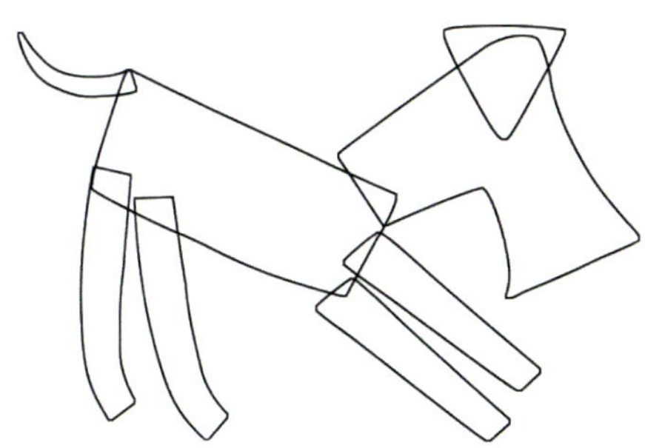

Draw a leaping cat

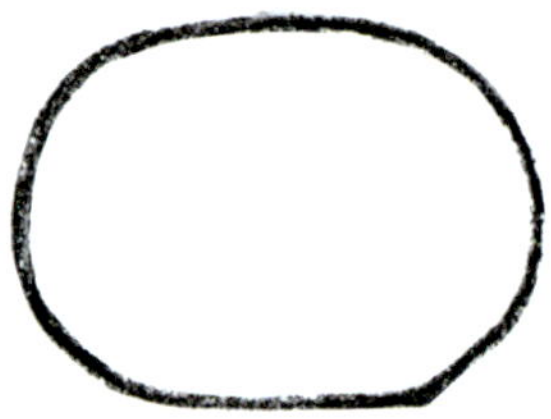

Draw lightly where lines overlap.

1 Draw the cat's head.

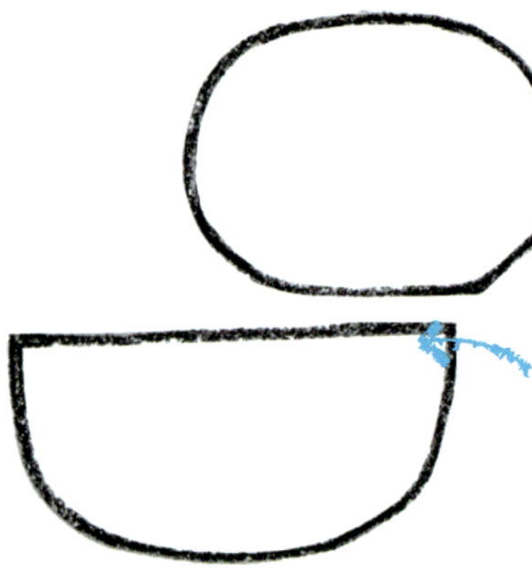

Leave a little gap for a collar later.

2 Add the body.

3 Now draw the ears.

4 Draw the legs.

5 Add a curved tail.

Color your cat with paints or colored pencils.

Add a little mouse too!

Make your cat look different!

Sitting up

Head at an angle

Tail the other way around

Add a collar or bow tie!

Straight legs

Draw a funny elephant

1 Draw the elephant's head.

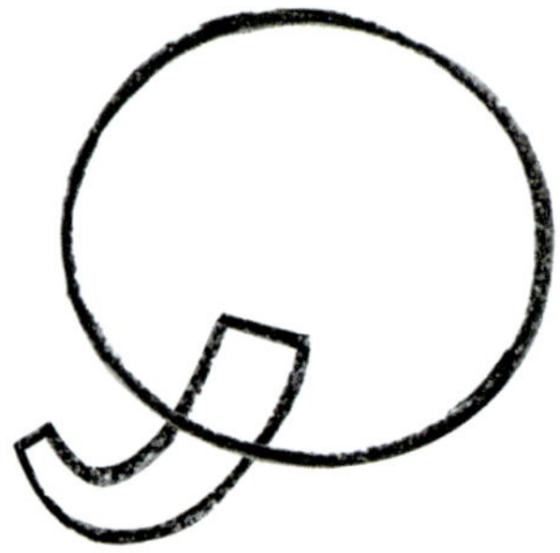

2 Add the elephant's trunk.

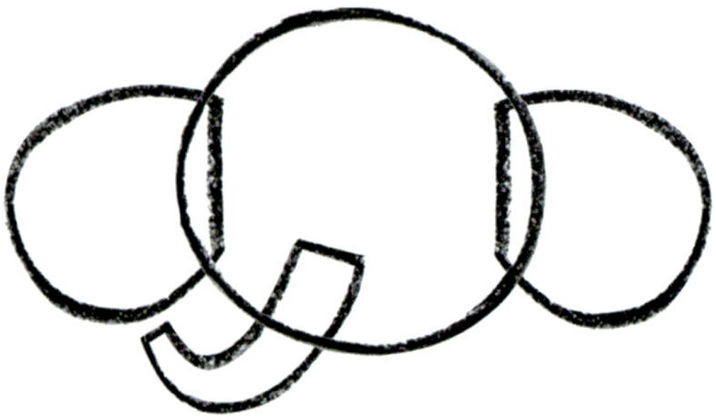

3 Draw ears on both sides.

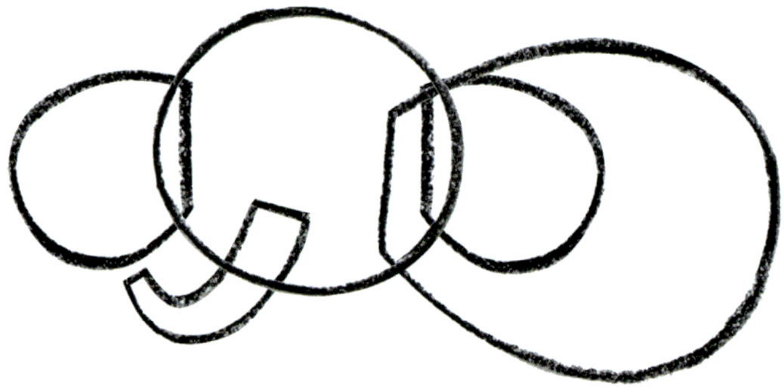

4 Now draw the body.

5 Draw the legs.

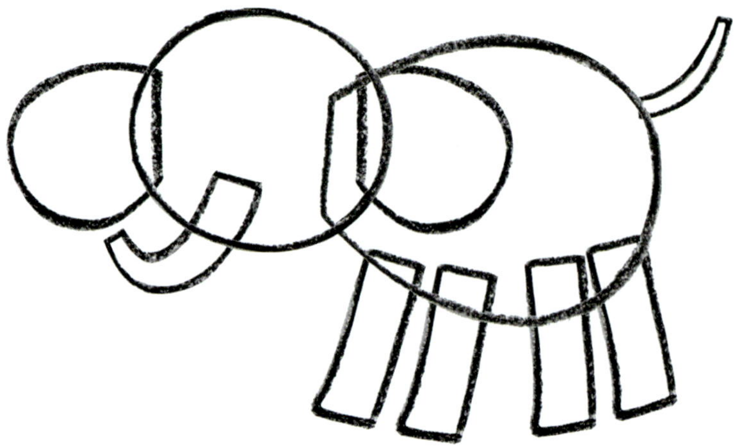

6 Add a swirly tail.

Color your elephant with paints or colored pencils.

You could make your elephant gray and pink.

Draw a baby elephant too!

Make your elephant look different!

You could draw the elephant standing up...

Just one ear showing

Just two legs showing

Draw a hat.

Draw a skater elephant!

Draw a flying bird

Draw lightly where lines overlap.

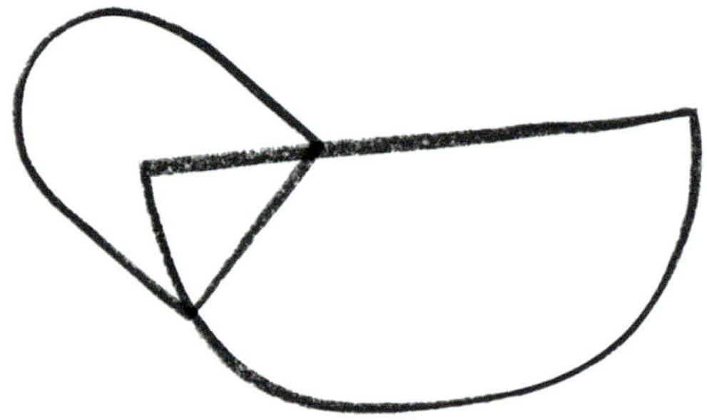

1 Draw the bird's head.

2 Add the body.

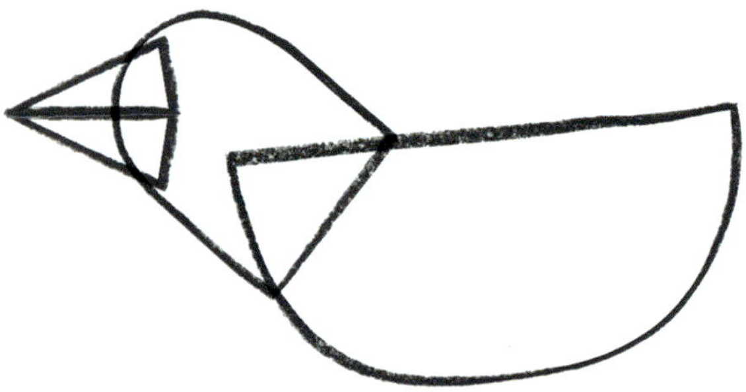

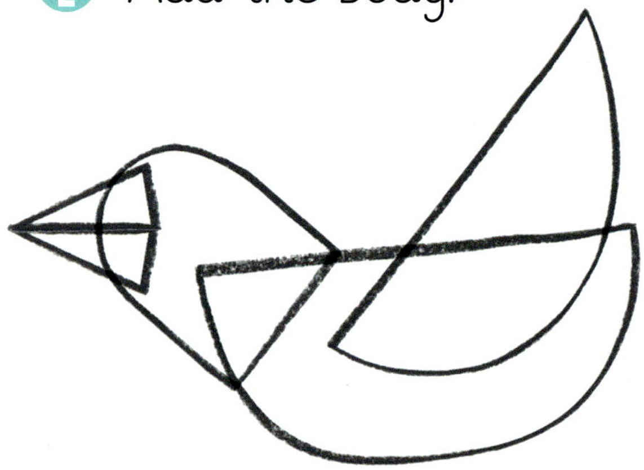

3 Now draw the beak.

4 Draw the wing.

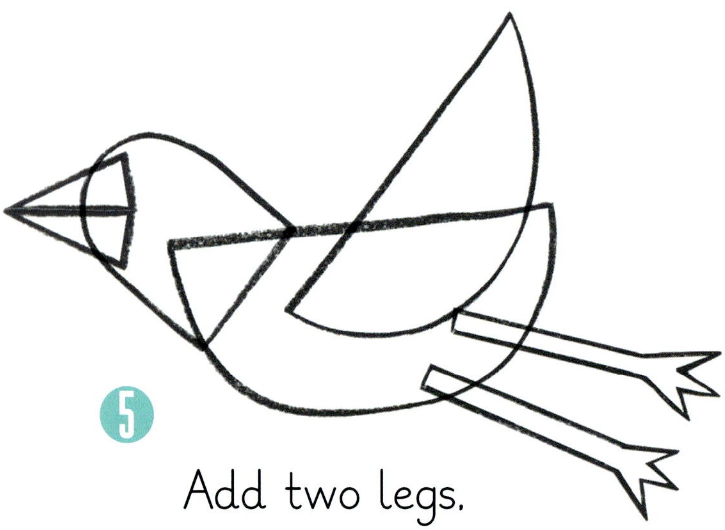

5 Add two legs.

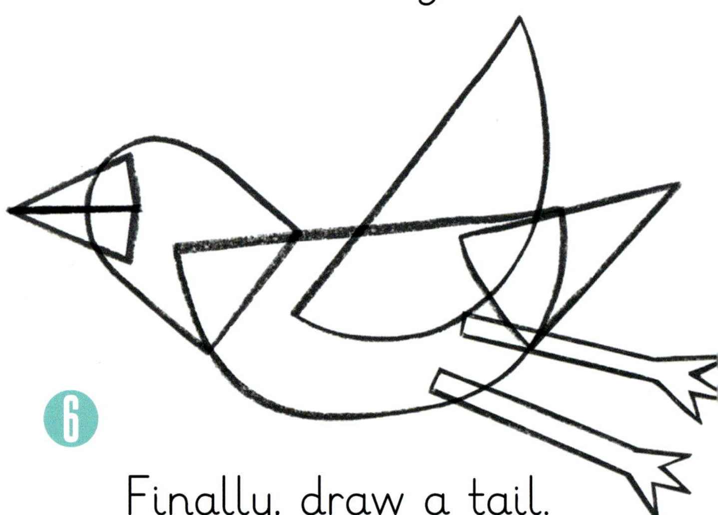

6 Finally, draw a tail.

Color your bird with paints or colored pencils.

Draw the eye with a dark center.

Make your bird look different!

Add a pretty flower!

Draw the beak open and eye closed.

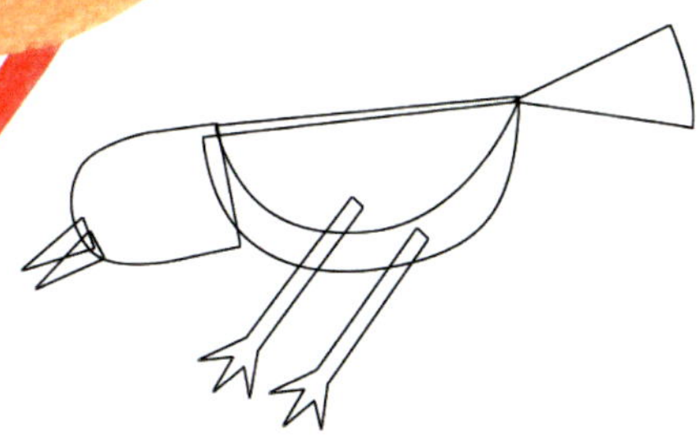

Legs and tail the other way around

Use the body shape twice to draw this bird.

Use spots and stripes.

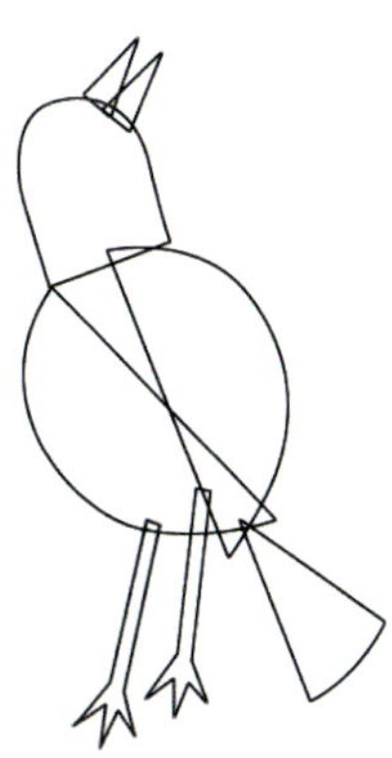

Straight legs

Draw a cute mouse

Notice the angle used to draw the head.

1 Draw the mouse's head.

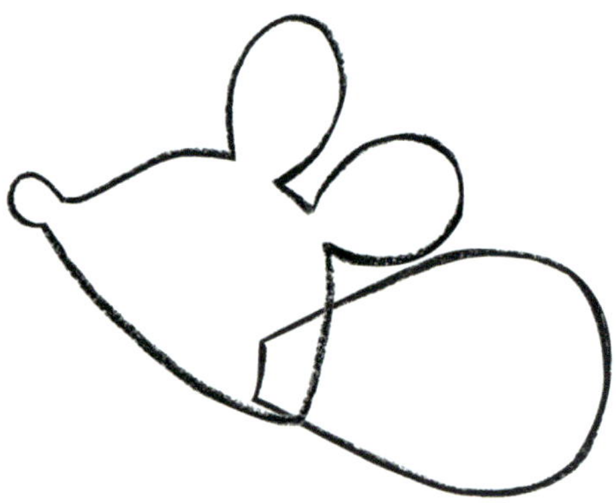

2 Next, draw the body.

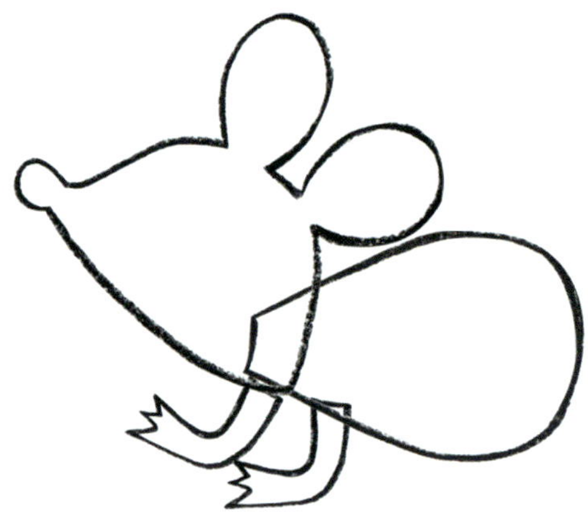

3 Add the front legs.

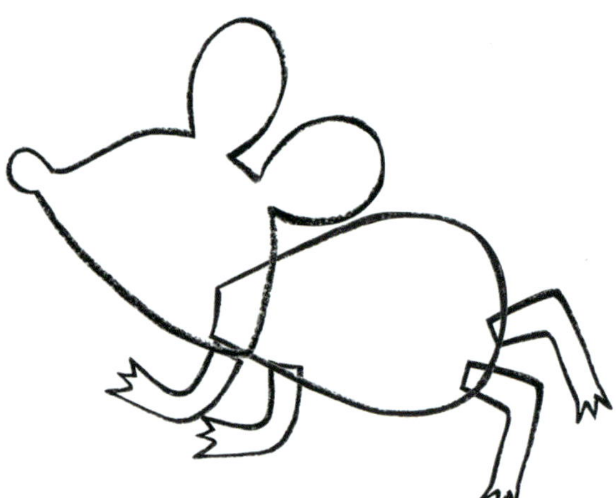

4 Draw the back legs.

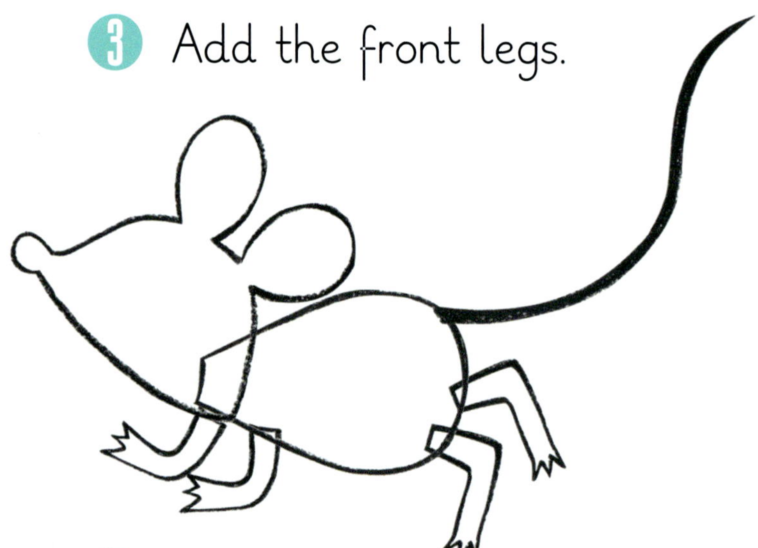

5 Now add the tail.

Draw a little friend!

Choose a color for the mouse's body and a different color for his face, ears, and paws.

Don't forget some whiskers!

Make your mouse look different!

He could be standing up with some cheese!

Draw a jacket and a bow tie to create a singing mouse.

Change the tail position if you draw the mouse standing.

Draw a lovely lion

Draw lightly where lines overlap.

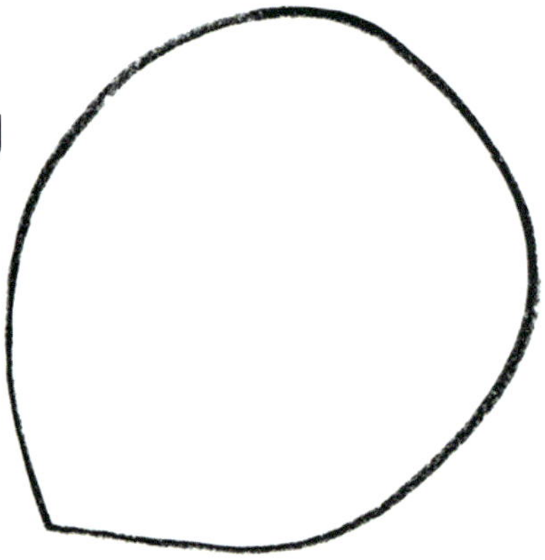

1 Draw the lion's head.

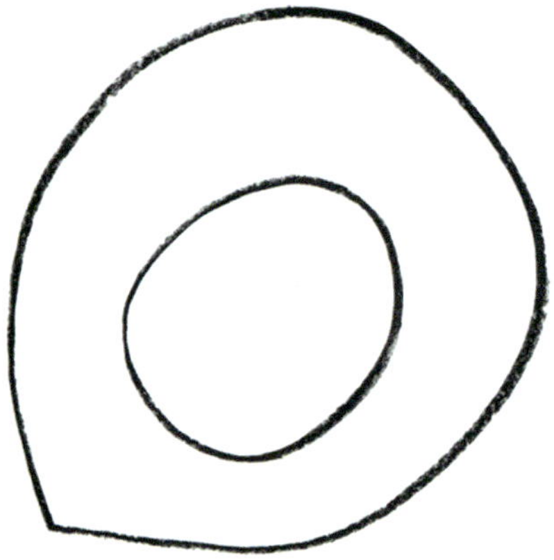

2 Draw his face next.

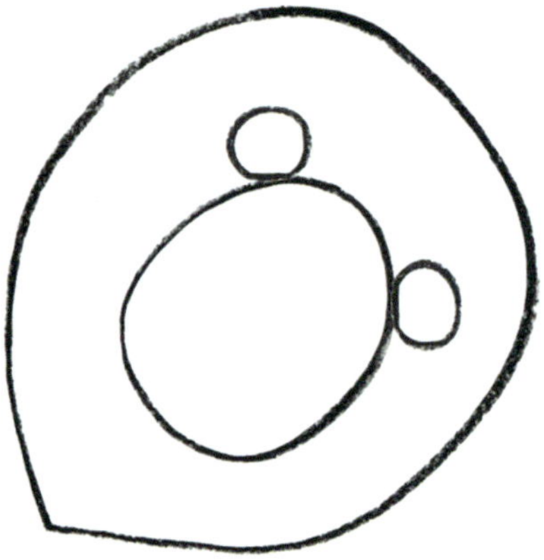

3 Now add the ears.

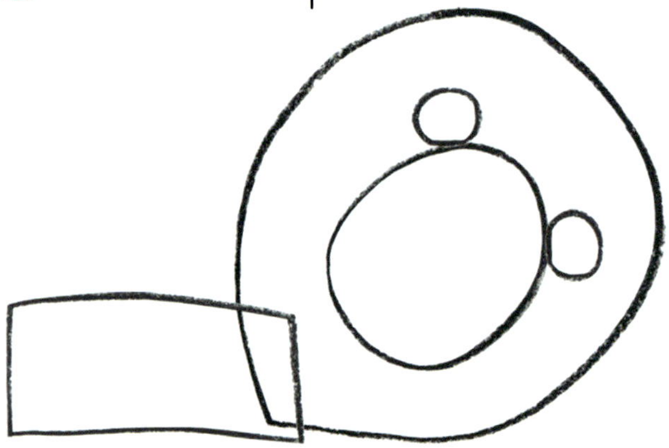

4 Now add the body.

5 Add the back legs and tail.

6 Draw the front legs.

Leave white gaps when you color the mane.

Add a little bird too!

Draw a happy face with long whiskers!

Make your lion look different!

Head at an angle

Draw a crown for the king of the jungle!

Turn the head around to make a fierce lion!

Straight legs

Sitting up

Draw a jolly giraffe

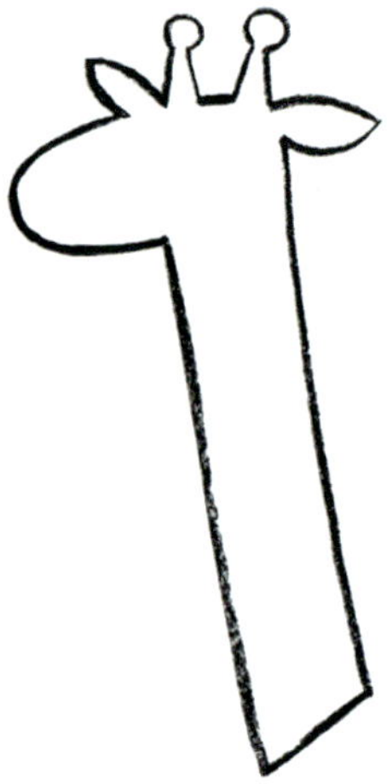

1 Draw the giraffe's head.

2 Now draw the body.

3 Draw the long legs.

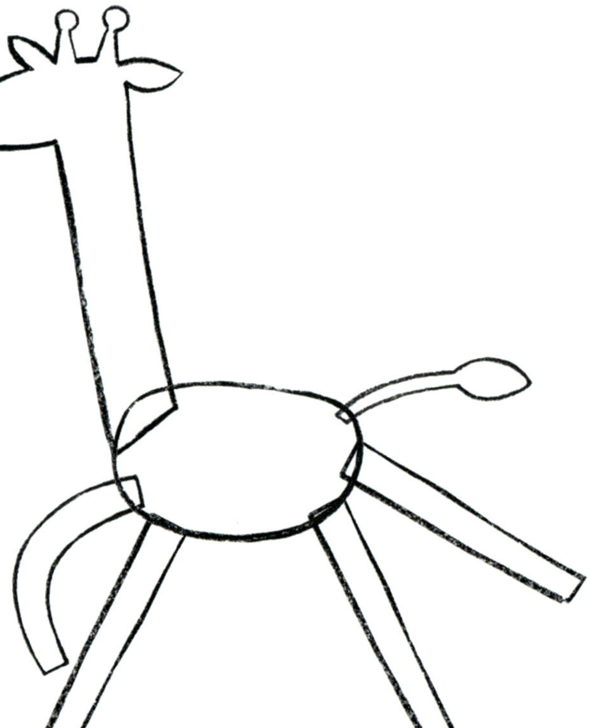

4 Add a bouncy tail.

Give your giraffe a camouflage effect with odd-shaped patterns.

Give the giraffe a lovely mane.

Add a friendly smile.

This giraffe has a pretty balloon!

Make the hooves darker.

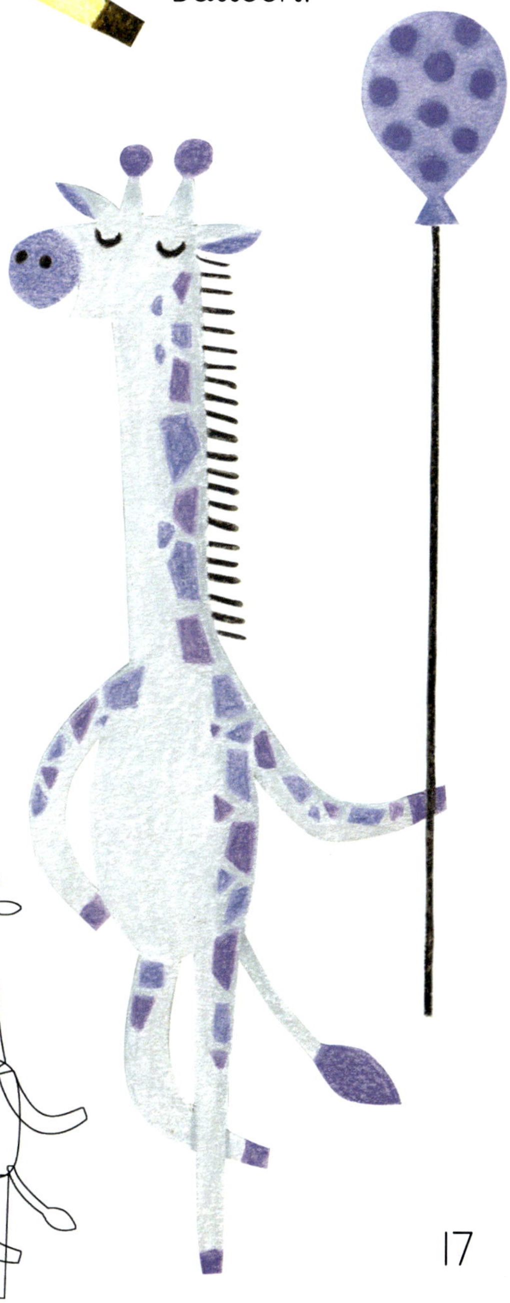

Make your giraffe look different!

Running giraffe

Add a sporty shirt!

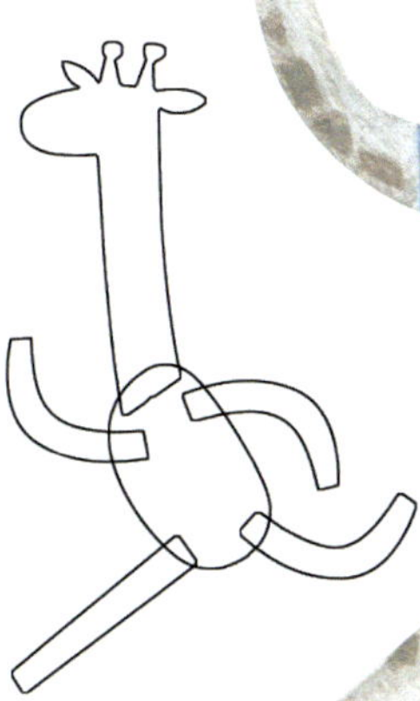

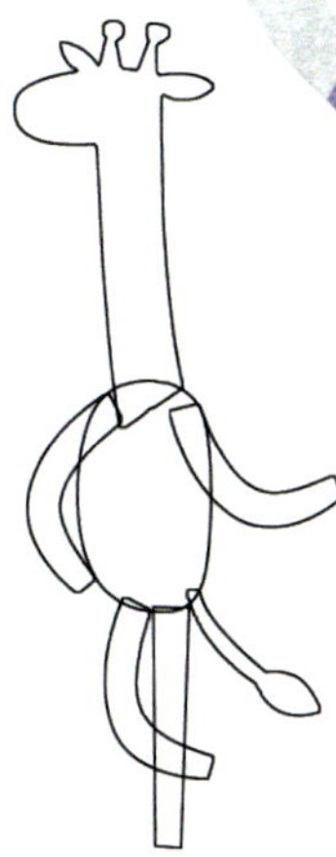

Draw the legs out wide.

Draw a sleepy owl

1 Draw the owl's head.

2 Add two tufts, like ears.

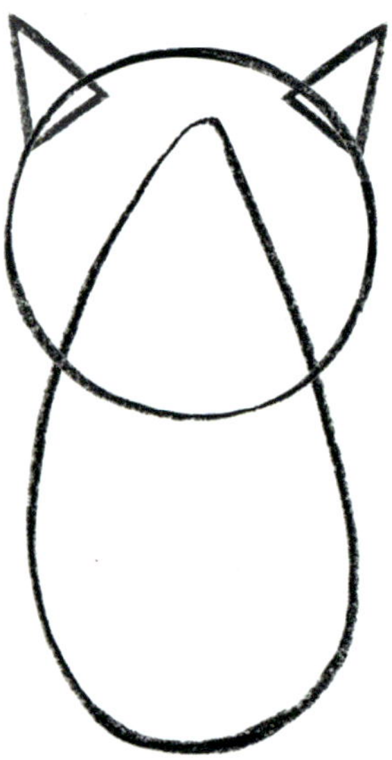

3 Now add the body.

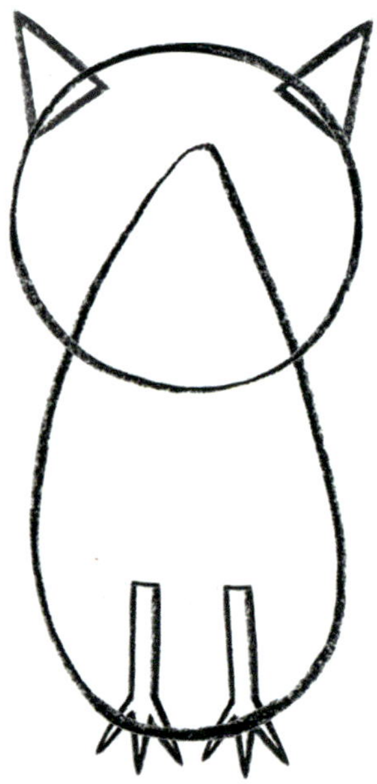

4 Draw the legs.

Draw the beak first and then draw the owl's eyes.

Draw one eye open and the other closed.

Make patterns for the feathers.

Add a tree branch for the owl!

Make your owl look different!

Professor Owl has a top hat and glasses!

Draw the body the other way up for these owls.

Draw a rocking horse

1 Draw the horse's head.

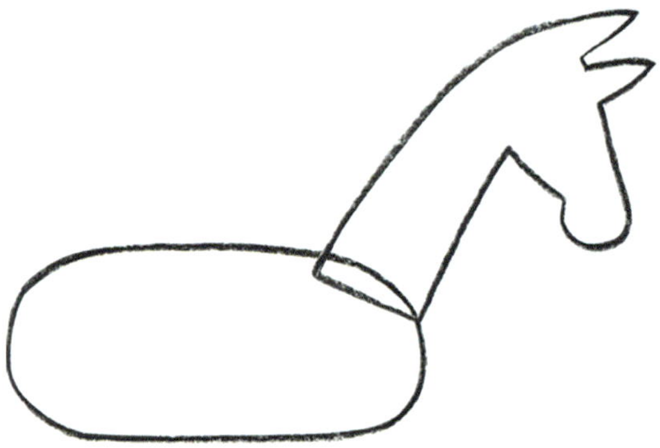

2 Add the body.

Draw lightly where lines overlap.

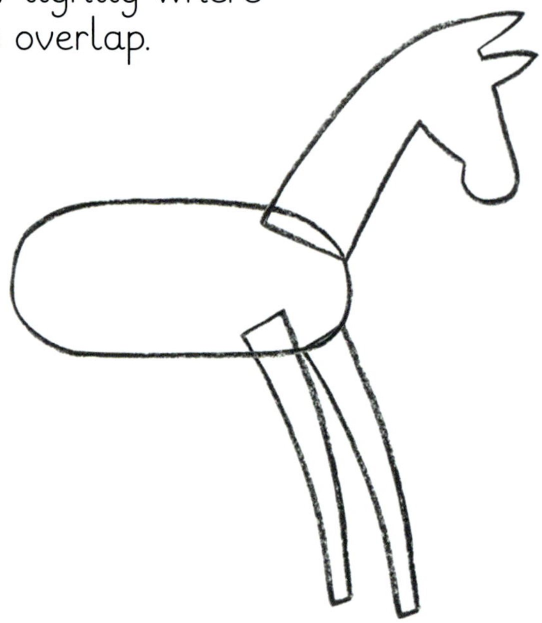

3 Now draw the front legs.

4 Draw the back legs.

5 Add a swooshing tail.

Make a pretty saddle with a star.

Draw a lovely mane too!

Draw along the edge of a large plate to create the rockers.

Make your horse look different!

Make the horse gallop by drawing the legs outstretched.

This horse is ready for a show!

Choose colors you like for your horse.

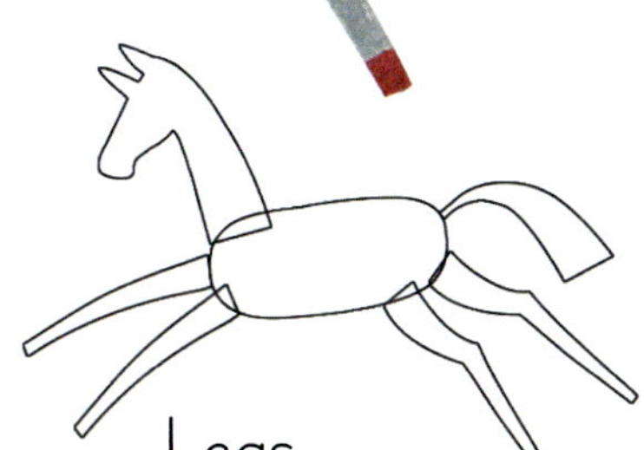

Legs outstretched

Straight legs

Draw a super squirrel

1 Draw the squirrel's head.

Draw lightly where lines overlap.

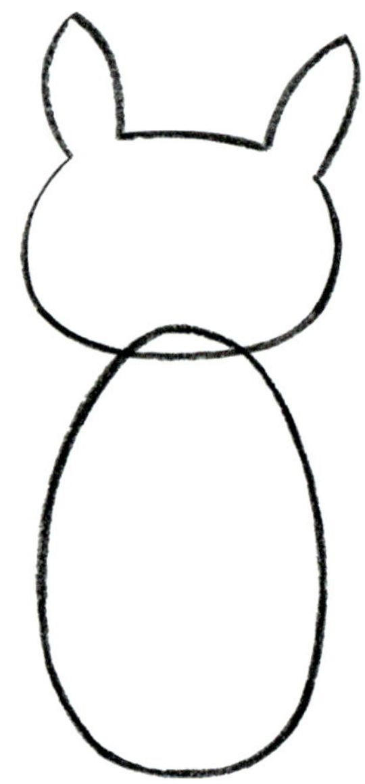

2 Now draw the body.

3 Add the arms and legs.

4 Then add a bushy tail.

Choose your favorite colors for your squirrel.

Leave white patches on his tummy, face, and ears.

Give your squirrel a tasty acorn in his paws!

Make your squirrel look different!

Head at an angle

You could make a squirrel smelling a flower!

Turn the body around to make this squirrel.

Draw a huge hippo

Draw lightly where lines overlap.

1 Draw the hippo's head.

2 Add the body.

3 Now draw the legs at different angles.

4 Add a little tail high up the hippo's back.

Give your hippo a bath by drawing water all around it!

Add a little bird too!

Make your hippo look different!

You can draw the hippo's mouth open without changing the shape of the head.

Draw closed eyes.

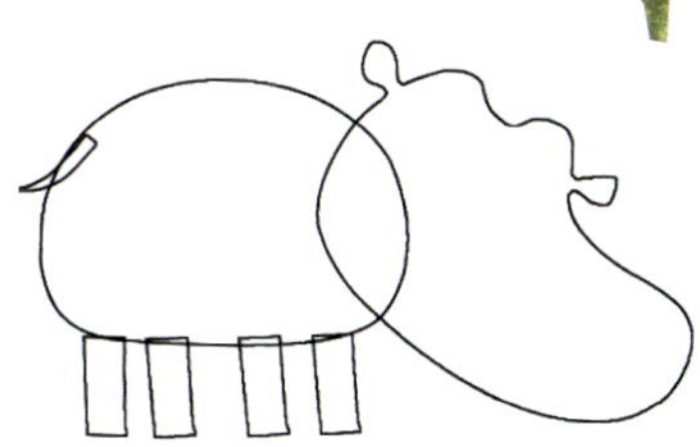

Just draw two legs and shift the head to draw this hippo!

Give the hippo a big smile!

Draw a colorful chameleon

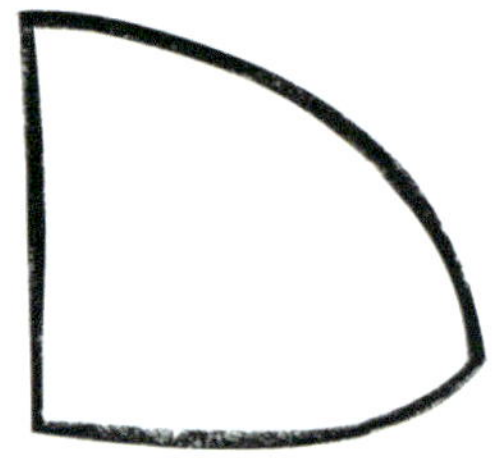

Draw lightly where lines overlap.

1 Draw the head first.

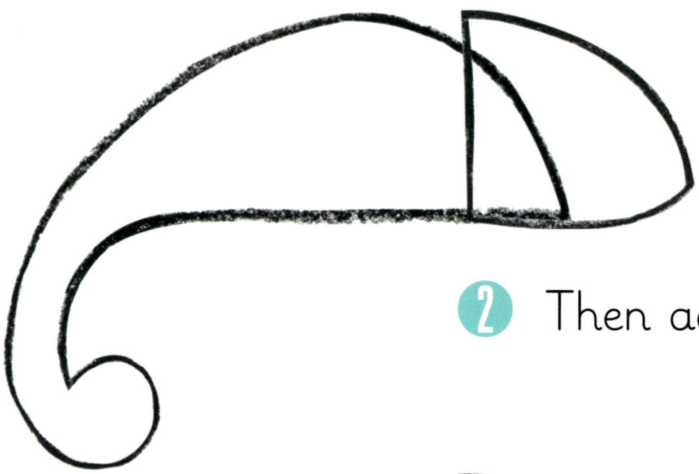

2 Then add the body.

3 Now draw the legs.

Draw a zigzag of spines along the back.

Draw a circle for the eye!

You could draw the eye in a spiral.

Put your chameleon on a branch with some bright green leaves.

Make your chameleon look different!

Add spikes on the head.

Give your chameleon a pattern!

Add a long, sticky tongue to catch lunch!

Don't forget that chameleons can change color, so create yours using your favorites!

Draw a hungry panda

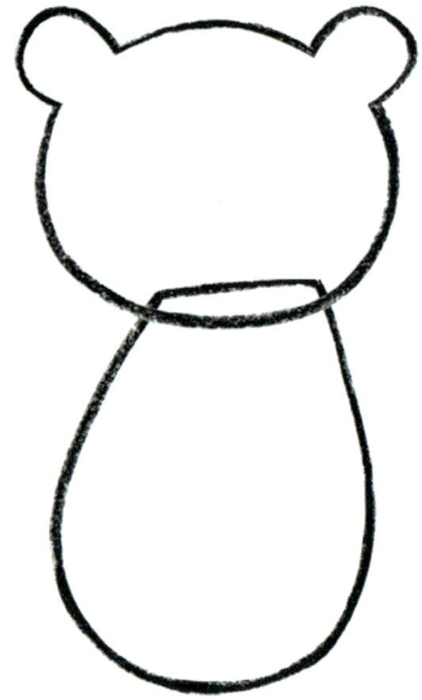

1. Draw the panda's head.
2. Add the body.

3. Now draw the arms.
4. Draw the legs.

Pandas like to eat bamboo shoots. You could give your panda a nice lunch!

Draw big black circles around the eyes.

Color the arms and legs black.

Draw claws on the paws!

Make your panda look different!

Add a friendly bird!

Give the panda a smile!

Draw a naughty monkey

1 Draw the monkey's head.

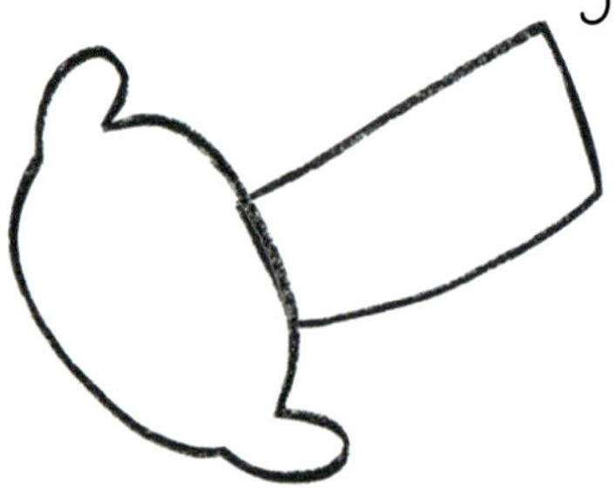

2 Add the body.

Draw lightly where lines overlap.

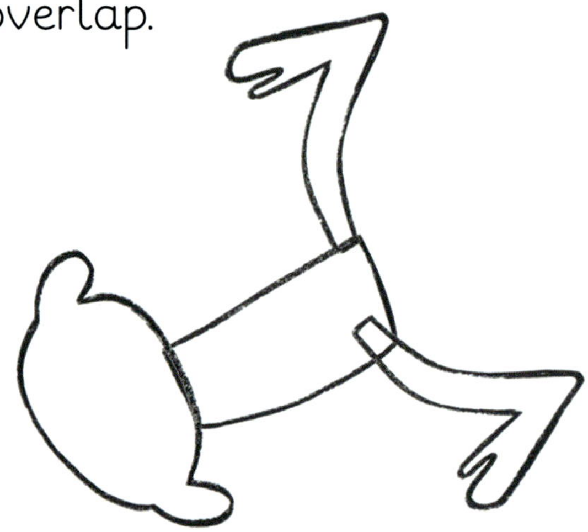

3 Now draw the legs.

4 Draw the monkey's arms.

5 Add a curly tail.

Make your monkey look different!

Add a buzzy bee!

Draw a tree for your monkey to play in!

You could give your monkey a hat!

Choose your favorite colors.

Make a pattern in the colors.

How about a musical monkey?

Draw a crazy creature!

You can invent your own crazy creatures by using shapes from different animals. Give your creature a funny name. Here's how to draw a Domolibird!

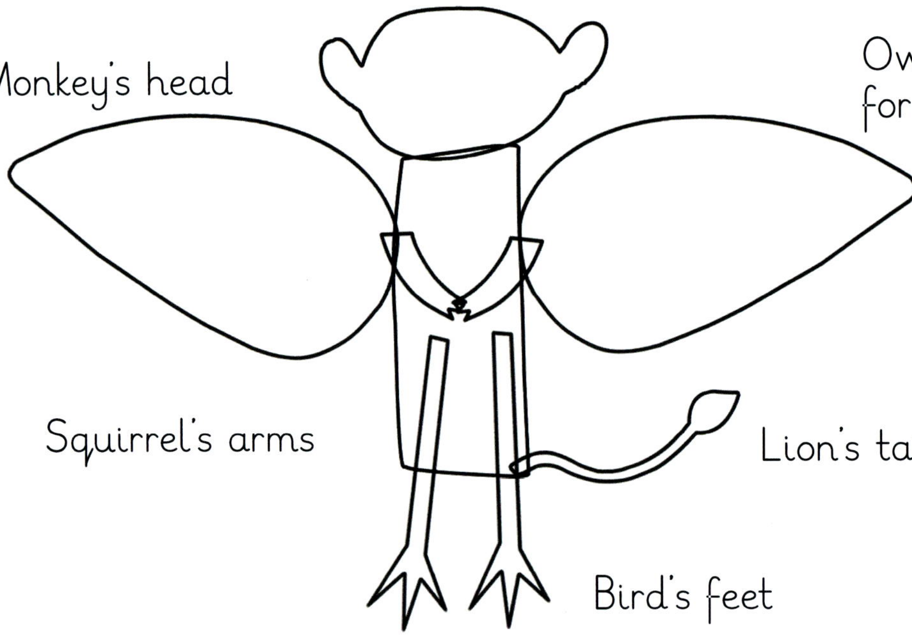

You could draw lots of different crazy creatures by mixing up the shapes in this book!

Make a display of all the animals you've drawn using this book. Impress your family and friends!